Uriel's Light

a nativity story

Tom Gavula

Uriel's Light: a nativity story

Copyright © 2022 Tom Gavula
Produced and printed by Stillwater River Publications. All rights reserved. Written and produced in the United States of America. This book may not be reproduced or sold in any form without the expressed, written permission of the author(s) and publisher.

Visit our website at ***www.StillwaterPress.com*** for more information.

First Stillwater River Publications Edition.

ISBN: 978-1-958217-23-8

1 2 3 4 5 6 7 8 9 10
Written by Tom Gavula.
Illustrations by Miranda Riccio.
Cover design by Lindsay Whelan.
Interior book design by Elisha Gillette.
Published by Stillwater River Publications, Pawtucket, RI, USA.

The views and opinions expressed in this book are solely those of the author(s) and do not necessarily reflect the views and opinions of the publisher.

For my parents,
whose lights cast my shadows.

"Every man during his life finds himself in regard to truth in the position of a man walking in the darkness with light thrown before him by the lantern he carries. He does not see what is not yet lighted up by the lantern; he does not see what he has passed which is hidden in the darkness; but at every stage of his journey he sees what is lighted up by the lantern, and he can always choose one side or the other of the road."

—Leo Tolstoy

Foreword

The biblical account of the birth of Jesus Christ has taught the citizens of the world about God's love for the human race, has strengthened the faith of Christian believers, and frequently restores hope to those who have lost their way on the journey of life. It has also been a source of inspiration for countless authors whose creative imaginations have produced heart-warming stories within the context of the Nativity of the Lord.

In *Uriel's Light*, Tom Gavula brings the reader back to the beloved town of Bethlehem through the inquisitive adventure of Uriel. The young and curious Uriel's determination to discover the source of a mysterious light grabbed my hand and led me back into that miraculous wonder of the first Christmas. It reawakened my own youthful, but dormant desire to be able to actually see and touch the infant in the manger.

What I especially found intriguing about reading *Uriel's Light*, is that this short story challenged me to become more aware of how I must always bring the light of Jesus Christ to others and never allow fear to extinguish that light. In addition, *Uriel's Light* has inspired me and should inspire you to do our best to be a light in the darkness. To be the light of courage, the light of kindness, the light of generosity, the light of hope, the light of service – that is Uriel's Light.

—Rev. David C. Procaccini

URIEL'S *Light*

Between Jerusalem and Hebron lay a smattering of tiny mountain hamlets. Hardly large enough to be called villages, each was a collection of several dwellings. Often the inhabitants were all family, extended family, and close friends who supported one another in this desert environment. The homes were built from what existed on the site. Walls were cobbled together using rough-hewn stone with clay mortar. Wood timbers supported a roof as well as the layers of clay-coated branches used to complete the covering. Mediterranean cypress, a narrow evergreen with dense foliage from ground to tip, grew straight and tall, and its trunk was particularly useful for constructing the roof of dwellings as well as fashioning door posts. Jerusalem pine, bushy when young, grew much taller and thrived in the arid conditions. A mature pine had a more massive bare trunk and an unkempt array of needled branches comprising its high canopy, which cast welcome shade. Its wood was prized for construction and its resin for making wine. In spite of the dusty and rugged conditions, life in this one cluster, called Peor, had a daily rhythm that kept the clan focused on the tasks necessary for community survival and support. This oneness of purpose brought an element of joy to what might otherwise seem like a dreary routine.

Uriel, barely a teenager and the youngest in one of the families, had not been feeling well of late. As the youngest, it was his job to shepherd the sheep and the few goats that they had. But because Uriel was sick, his older brother, Taoma, after working with their father in the morning, took the herd off to where they would graze for the night and the following day. The land was arid and grazing meadows dotted the countryside in the valleys between the hills. Taoma and Uriel knew the region well, and over the years had developed a judicious and systematic sequence that hit all the good grazing spots and never allowed any to be over-grazed. Taoma did not mind filling in for his brother; he found shepherding to be a respite from the harder work his father had him doing all day. He got to leave his father early to tend the herd. He enjoyed working with his father, they got along well, but a change in the routine was always welcome.

After eating his evening meal—a stew his mother made with lentils, beans, leeks, cucumber, and garlic, plus some dried fish and warm bread—Uriel was feeling much better. His boyish energy had returned, and he begged his mother to let him go join Taoma with the flock. Observing how his appetite had returned, she knew he had recovered from whatever ailed him. But mothers like to take things slower than teenage boys, so she was still wary.

"Uriel, you've been sick for two days. Give yourself

time to recover your strength. Tomorrow, if you are still feeling well, you can take the sheep."

"But Mother, I'm fine. I've slept all day and if I stay here, I'll just be staring at the ceiling all night. Besides, Taoma can stay there with me tonight. He won't mind. He and I don't get to spend much time together. Please, Mother?"

"Oh Uriel, I suppose if I don't let you go, you'll be nothing but a pest all evening. Go, but make sure that Taoma stays with you tonight. He can return in the morning and then go help your father. You know which pasture he's taken the herd to, I suppose?"

"Yes, I told him where to go."

"Well let me fill your scrip before you leave without anything to eat in the morning. And don't forget your lantern; it's already dark. And your aba, take your aba; it might get cold tonight. If I didn't remind you, you'd just run off with nothing." His mother had made the aba for him just last year. Having made one previously for her husband and for Taoma, she was particularly proud of her work on Uriel's. Woven primarily of camel's hair, it served as a waterproof covering should it rain and as a nice warm blanket when he slept under the stars. She skillfully crafted it so he could easily secure it about his shoulders and keep his hands free. One day she would modify the other two and incorporate features she had put into Uriel's.

Uriel loved being the shepherd. To him, every day

was an adventure. But it was not all fun and games; he took his responsibilities very seriously, conscientiously watching the herd and planning when and where to move to the next grazing area. Taoma had taught him well and both boys, young men really, made their parents proud.

Uriel left his house with the scrip full of food, his wineskin full of water, camel-hair aba to keep him warm at night and dry should it rain, and his staff and lantern. The sun had set an hour ago and it was dark. As Uriel walked along, he realized that he had not lit his lantern but could see his way with no problem. The moon, although only a bit more than half-full, was bright and the sky was cloudless. The dense, milky band of stars stretched across the sky from horizon to horizon. To Uriel, the lantern was just excess baggage that he didn't need, so he hurried back to his house and placed it on the ground by the door. He considered doing the same with his aba but decided that would make his mother too angry should she see it there. With the wineskin and scrip of food slung over his shoulder and the aba tied around his waist, he could wield his staff as if conquering the world, and he felt totally liberated. As he walked and jogged and skipped along, he suddenly became aware that he had a companion. His moon-shadow was to his right and slightly ahead. It accompanied him, barely visible, but was glued to his feet and not to be cast off. It had a life of its own as it undulated over the rocky terrain, one minute gliding along the flat ground, at other times seeming to jump up as it slid from ground to boulder and back down again, and occasionally standing upright as a mini-Uriel against a dense cypress tree. Uriel was comforted by it.

Everything seemed dreamlike in the ashen moonlight. The rocks and bushes themselves, which made up the monochrome gray landscape on either side of the road, seemed to rise up from the ground as specters, trailing their ephemeral shadows. Were they being borne up from the earth to eventually develop into matter more solid, or were they retreating back into the soil from whence they came? Either way, in the dim light they seemed now caught in a halfway state of near reality. And all was quiet. Normally the night has its own sounds if you listen closely. Nocturnal insects, birds, and mammals break the silence of the night with their own language. But tonight, all was still and quiet. Was it the brightness of the moon that had them fooled into thinking that their time of night had not yet come? Or did it perhaps portend a change in the weather? The night can be read by those attuned to it, and typically Uriel was very attuned. But tonight, he was oblivious and travelled along without a care in the world.

The pasture he was heading for was a few miles away. Although not directly adjacent to the road, he knew even in the pale moonlight that he would locate the landmarks which would tell him to veer off the road and up into the surrounding hills. Every so often in his peripheral vision he would sense some movement. But each time he'd turn his head toward the motion it would be gone. Likely a hare or a foraging hedgehog. Nothing that worried him. To Uriel, it was a game to see if he could catch a glimpse of the animal and identify it before it melted into the darkness. Fallow deer were common, but usually they would remain as frozen statues when someone passed along the road. Only if you advanced toward them would they scurry off. He wondered how many such deer he had already passed unaware.

The landmark he sought was a particular grouping of cypress trees. Once Uriel reached the spot he headed up into the surrounding hills. At first, he had to peck his way very carefully as the large rocks and scrub bushes were like vague apparitions, often seeming to conspire against him and spring forth from the earth in an attempt to block his way or trip him up. But Uriel was light on his feet and easily navigated the gauntlet until finally arriving at smoother ground. Up into the mountain meadow he went, listening carefully for the sound of the sheep. Several young lambs and kids were in the herd, and they would call to their mother who would answer back to give reassurance that she was near. He was surprised that he could not hear them yet. Then off in the distance something caught his eye. It was a faint glow on the horizon to the north. It had not been visible from down on the road, but now that he was up higher he could see it. He stopped and stared at it, but it was too far off to tell what it was. It must be a fire, but it would need to be a large one to create the glow he was seeing. Perhaps Taoma would know what it is.

Uriel continued up the slope and eventually heard the sound of a kid calling for its mother. Normally some older sheep and goats would be on the alert for predators and would call to the shepherd when they sensed movement nearby. But the herd was familiar with Uriel and his scent. Hence, when he finally arrived, he found his brother asleep. He thought about scaring Taoma but didn't want to anger him. The strange light in the distance had piqued his curiosity and he might need his brother's help and cooperation in order to investigate it. So, gently he shook his brother's shoulder and called his name.

Even so, Taoma woke with a start and had his staff in hand in the blink of an eye. But as quickly as he reacted, he relaxed again at the sight of his brother.

"What are you doing here? I could have felled you with my staff."

"I know. Next time I'll throw a rock at you from a distance."

"Very funny. Does Mother know you came?"

"Of course she knows. I was feeling much better and convinced her to let me come."

"You mean you tormented her until she gave in."

"Well, sort of. And she said to tell you to stay out here with me tonight."

"Good, because if I headed back now, I wouldn't get much sleep before having to go off with Papa. But now with you here I probably won't get much sleep anyway."

"Hey, Taoma, did you notice that light over there?"

"What light? I don't see any light."

"Oh wait, you can't see it from here; that hill is in the way. Come on down here further and I'll show you."

They did not need to retreat very far down the slope before the distant glow was visible. Taoma was immediately certain about the source.

"It must be a fire. What else could it be?"

"That's what I was thinking but what could be burning? I'm going to go check it out. It can't be all that far."

"Uriel, you can't go wandering off in the dark not knowing how far it is or where you'll end up. Mother would kill me if I let you go."

"Oh, come on, Taoma. It can't be all that far away. Besides, I take the sheep to pastures in that direction all the time so it's not like I'll get lost or something. And with this moonlight I can be there and back in no time. Don't you want to know what it is?"

"Sure, I'm curious. It does look awfully strange. But I can't let you go wandering off alone. What if there's some sort of trouble there?"

"Okay, then you go, and I'll stay here."

"I'm not going anywhere except back to sleep."

"Then as soon as you fall asleep, I'm going."

"No wonder Mother let you come out here tonight.

You just never take 'no' for an answer. You're going to go no matter what I say or do. Just remember, I never agreed to you going."

"Thanks, Taoma. I won't be long. I promise"

Leaving his aba and staff behind so he could travel with unencumbered ease, Uriel set out to investigate. He made his way back down to the road, but once there, he no longer had a view of the distant light. However, he knew that the road ahead went uphill, and he expected he would again be able to see his destination once he reached the top. Just as expected, when he crested the hill, the glow was clearly visible. It was a peculiar light. If it were a fire, he would have expected it to dance and change in intensity, but this was like a light frozen in place. Also, at least from this distance, he could detect no smoke, nothing obscuring the stars above the light. The closer he got the more curious he became.

So far, Uriel knew this area well. But he was approaching the outer limit of his normal grazing pastures. Suddenly he heard the faint sound of a cowbell and saw a dim light. Someone was approaching him on the road. It was not unusual for people to travel at night and avoid the heat of the day. Taking a lesson from the deer in such circumstances, Uriel always moved quickly off the path twenty cubits or so, crouched down, and remained completely still until the other person passed. In this case, it was a man leading his ox and on his way to who knows where. It was generally safe travelling at night, but Uriel was always cautious and would always blend into the landscape rather than risk the interaction, provided he had enough time. Even if the other travelers sensed his initial movement, they would likely conclude he was just an animal more afraid of the encounter than they were. At times the person might stop and stare into the darkness where they thought they had seen something, but he was never detected. Or if they did see him, they were as eager to move away as he was to resume his trek.

Once the man and his ox passed, Uriel stuck to the road for as long as he could but then came to the point where he would need to head up into the hills in order to reach the light. Just as he had done to reach his brother, Uriel headed east and threaded his way through the rocks and bushes, climbing up to the furthest meadow that he frequented. Up in the meadow, the going was easier, but the light he was chasing was further to the north. He pictured himself grazing the herd there and tried to remember what was off in that direction. All he could recall was a mountain. Near the base of the mountain there was the small town of Bethlehem, much larger than where he lived but with similar houses. Beyond that was the city limits of Jerusalem. But the light was definitely not as far off as the city, rather, it seemed to emanate from what he thought was the mountain area.

Uriel turned north and headed across the pasture

keeping the light directly in front of him. As soon as he did so, something worrying caught his attention. Not only did he see it, but he felt it in the change of air temperature. He froze in his tracks and a feeling of dread welled up inside of him. He should have noticed it much sooner, but his focus had always been ahead and to the right. Now, looking straight ahead toward his destination, the peripheral vision on his left picked up on the approaching blackness. As if black ink had been spilled in the heavens and was steadily flowing across the sky, a dense line of thick clouds stretched across the sky. Where the clouds had advanced, there was nothing but pitch-blackness; all the starlight was obliterated. Very shortly it would cover the moon and the light he had been relying on would be gone. Without his lantern he would be blind and finding his way would be nearly impossible. Had he noticed sooner he would have retreated back to his brother and hunkered down there for the night. But he had gone too far for that to be a possibility now. His only option was to hurry to the light he was chasing before the moonlight was gone and then wait until dawn before heading back. He now understood why the night was so quiet. The animals knew that a dramatic change in the weather was coming, and they had all prepared well in advance. He and Taoma were savvy enough to read the signs but had simply dismissed them. A lesson learned. Uriel hoped that he would not pay too high a price.

Heading to the light with a new determination, he covered ground quickly. Just as quickly the clouds swallowed up the moon. As luck would have it though, Uriel was now close enough to the light that it actually provided him with as much visibility as the moonlight had. Up ahead he saw the shear white face of a high limestone cliff. The luminous glow was concentrated at its base but reflected off the gray-white rock face and brightened the landscape for a considerable distance. It was this reflection of light off the escarpment that enabled it to be seen from a long distance. As Uriel got closer, he could see that there was a sizable cave cut into the mountainside, and it was from this cave that the light originated.

Limestone caves were common in the region. They were created by water seeping into the soft stone, eroding it over time, resulting in fissures and caves. Animals loved to occupy these places and make a den for their family. People did the same with larger caves, often enlarging them by hand to make a more suitable dwelling for either themselves or often for their livestock. Uriel and Taoma knew of many such caves and utilized them for shelter from time to time.

Uriel could hear the bleating of sheep and see a sizable herd around the outside of the cave. No one challenged him as he advanced. Standing at the entrance and facing inward was a man who appeared to be the shepherd. He suddenly sensed Uriel's approach, turned slightly to acknowledge Uriel, almost as if he was expected, and then refocused his gaze inside. More like a large hollow in the rock than a typical cave, the entrance was wide, almost as wide as the cave itself. It appeared to have been fashioned to provide a shelter for someone's animals and a place where they could feed out of the hot sun or bad storms. Uriel stepped inside, and directly in front of him stood an ox and a donkey, seemingly asleep on their feet. Off to his right, back in the most sheltered corner of the cave, stood a young man. Bearded and having a weary but resolute look on his face, the man noted Uriel's presence. Beside the man, sitting cross-legged on a pile of hay on the cave floor, was a woman with a baby at her breast. She reminded Uriel of his teenage cousin. Her eyes were focused intently on her child as she gently stroked his head. But then she raised her head, looked straight into Uriel's eyes, and gave him the most loving smile he had ever seen. The entire scene had him mesmerized, and like the shepherd, he just stood there soaking it all in.

Having had its fill, the baby quickly fell asleep in the woman's arms. She held the child for a few minutes and then handed the baby to the man. He gently placed the infant on the straw in the animals' feeding trough beside the woman. Suddenly Uriel, as if waking from a trance, thought about the light. There was no fire lit to keep them warm and yet the entire chamber was filled with light. There was no source that he could identify but it did seem to emanate from the corner where the young family rested. It was a light like no other he had ever seen: a soft, golden glow that sprang from around the manger and literally spilled out of the cave and skyward up the mountain face. It was like a river of light, an eternal spring, flowing from out of thin air.

Uriel's wonder clearly showed on his face. The woman looked at him knowingly and beckoned him to come. He came to her and stood staring at the sleeping baby.

"What is your name?" she asked.

"Uriel."

"Nice to meet you, Uriel. My name is Myriam, this is my husband, Yosef, and the baby is Yeshu. Isn't he beautiful?"

Uriel's tongue was frozen. He had trouble thinking clearly let alone speaking.

"Are you here alone, Uriel?"

"Yes."

Myriam smiled, knowing that he hardly knew how to process what he was seeing.

"Yes. I went to meet my brother with the sheep and saw the light in the distance. He didn't want me to go but I had to come and see. At first I thought something was on fire."

"Well, you're a brave young man to come here alone at night. Thank you for coming."

"May I touch the baby?"

"Certainly."

Uriel gently stroked the infant's cheek and the baby, eyes remaining closed, seemed to smile ever so slightly. Uriel knelt at the side of the trough, crossed his arms along its edge, and with his chin on his arms just stared at the sleeping baby. How long he stayed there he couldn't say, but eventually he sat down on the ground and looked about the cave. The couple had very few possessions there with them, and he wondered how they came to be there, especially with a newborn. Myriam seemed to read his mind. Somehow mothers always seem to know what children are thinking.

"The inns were all full in Bethlehem. The landowner directed us here so that we would at least have some shelter for the night. It will do until we can find someplace better tomorrow."

"But a storm is coming, and this won't give much protection from the cold and wind. The baby is so tiny."

Then Uriel remembered the scrip full of food slung over his shoulder, and the warm coat that he left with his brother. He thought how much they needed that coat more than he did.

"Would you like something to eat? I've had plenty. It's just some bread that my mother made and dried fruit."

"That's very kind of you, Uriel. I'll have just a little."

Uriel handed her the pouch of snacks that his mother had packed but he wanted to do more. He now regretted leaving his aba behind; it would provide a nice warm covering for mother and baby. He decided to go back and get it. And in typical Uriel fashion, once he made up his mind to do something there was no stopping him. Without any preamble he suddenly jumped to his feet, shouted, "I'll be right back," and ran out in a flash. His mind envisioned the entire route. Straight across from the cave to the meadow, then right down to the road, then back to the cypress cluster and up to the herd. Now that he knew the route, he would make it there and back in no time flat. He weaved in and out among the rocks and brush as if his feet knew exactly where to step and quickly reached the field. Then between the field and the road, more rocks, trees, and brambles to navigate, but again he managed it with remarkable ease. Once on the road it headed downhill, and when it eventually leveled out the cave was well out of view. He stopped to catch his breath, sat on a rock by the roadside, and had a drink of water from his wineskin.

Then suddenly it dawned on him. Uriel looked straight up, and it was like looking into a black abyss. There was nothing for him to even focus his eyes on except one small spot off to his west that was just ever so slightly a different shade of dark. Struggle as it might, the moonlight had lost its battle and couldn't shine through. With no lantern he should not be able to see a thing. Once beyond the light of the cave how had he been able to find his way down to the road and then along the pathway to this point? And yet he could see.

Similar to when the moon was shining, he was able to discern the stones and shrubbery and the edge of the road. But the tint of this light differed from moonlight. Although very faint, it reminded him of the light in the cave by its soft golden hue. But what was its source?

Uriel got up and slowly moved further down the road. He was wary now and confused. As he walked, he pivoted around in a full circle looking for the source of the light, but it seemed to have no source. It just was. Then standing in one spot he rotated around slowly, eyes looking straight into the distance. All was pitch black and undiscernible, as if no world existed beyond where he stood. But when he looked down, he was able to see the road and just enough ahead to navigate. He continued on, and the path ahead remained always vaguely illuminated. The light stayed with him. Looking over his shoulder and behind, he saw nothingness. Again, he stopped, looked all about, and examined his clothes. Then suddenly he saw it. There, stuck to his tunic sleeve, was a piece of straw, probably from when he rested his arms on the side of the trough. He concluded that somehow that piece of hay must carry with it the light from the cave. He grabbed it in his hand so as not to lose it and then headed off down the road. It didn't make sense. He couldn't explain it. But neither could he explain the light in the cave. It just was.

When he reached the cypress trees, he headed up to the pasture, easily navigating his way. When he got there, he found Taoma snoring. Typical of his brother. Off in the distance, in the direction of the cave, Uriel observed a strange sight. When he was here previously there was no evidence of the light from this location. Now, the light from the cave gave the dense clouds over that distant spot an eerie glow, like nothing he had ever seen before. It was sure to attract attention from far and wide.

Rather than wake Taoma, Uriel grabbed his aba and headed back down. There would be plenty of time later to tell everything to Taoma, but for now, he was still single-mindedly on his mission. Still marveling but not questioning, he used the light from the straw to show him the way, and the trip seemed even shorter each time he covered the route. Then, nearly to the crest of the hill on the road, after which he would head up to that far pasture and then over to the cave, he heard voices. Someone was coming, and they were fairly close. The hilly terrain had prevented him from seeing their lantern, and now they were nearly on top of him. In a panic, he leapt over some rocks, stumbled over some others, and then crouched down behind a small shrub. He closed his eyes and held his breath. From their voices he could tell they were two men, and likewise he could tell that they had seen something. Almost exactly at the spot where he left the road, they stopped, and he could hear them whispering to each other. *Do they see me?* he wondered. *Are they out to rob me?* So many frightful thoughts raced through his mind. It seemed like forever before they resumed speaking out loud and continued on their way.

Uriel remained paralyzed there until he was certain the men were far enough away. Then he opened his eyes and took a long deep breath. He felt like he had been holding his breath the entire time. But when he went to move, he discovered that he couldn't see. All was pitch black. In his panic he had dropped the sprig of hay and there was no finding it now. He felt on the ground immediately around him but to no avail. So close to completing his mission, he wondered what to do now. From where he was right now, he could head up to the far pasture and then eventually the cave light would be enough to let him see the way. But how to get that far? There was only one way. So, slowly, crouching down so he could feel ahead with both arms and hands extended, he painstakingly inched his way up the slope. At one point he brushed against a thorny bush and got two long bloody scratches on his arm. His hands kept hitting into rocks and small boulders until they were bruised and raw, and his knees were skinned and bleeding. But ever so slowly he was making progress. Several times he had to stop and take a drink because it felt like he was eating dust. From rock to rock and rock to bush he shuffled along until finally the rocks thinned out and he felt that he was at the lower edge of the meadow. There he rested for a spell and tried to gather himself for what he felt would be the easier final stretch.

Once he was physically and mentally ready, he stood up. He felt he could walk upright through the pasture and then beyond the pasture and toward the cave. He hoped to have just enough cave-light to be able to navigate. He took one step, slammed his left toe into a rock and fell to the ground crying in pain. Tears came to his eyes, and it was quite a while before the pain subsided enough for Uriel to continue on. The pasture still had outcropping rocks, so he had to continue very slowly and carefully. His toe throbbed, knees were scraped, arm was scratched and bloody, and his hands were raw.

Finally, there was enough cave-light reflecting off the rock face that he could see without a problem. When he reached the cave there were many more people there who had been attracted to the light, but they all stood back near the entrance and gave the family their space. They spoke quietly among themselves and were in wonder at the sight. Uriel ducked and weaved between them and approached the mother. The baby had been in her arms, and she was just placing him back down into the trough of hay.

Uriel's tunic hid his battered knees and the cuts on his arm, but Myriam noticed his bloody toe. The toenail was partially ripped off and dried blood mixed with dirt was caked on the end of his sandal.

"Uriel, what did you do to your toe? Go and wash it off."

He had gotten used to the pain and it wasn't until now that he saw how ugly the wound was. He went outside the cave and poured some water from his wineskin on it to wash off the dirt and then went back in.

"I brought my aba to cover the baby. It's camelhair and very warm. You can have it."

"Why, thank you, Uriel, that's so very kind. Would you like to cover him? You may if you like."

Uriel gently stretched the coat over the manger and the baby. Then, as he had done before, he softly stroked the infant's cheek with a fingertip. As soon as he had done that the throbbing of his toe stopped and, as he would discover later, the scratches and scrapes on his knees and arm disappeared. For a minute or so he continued to rub the baby's soft skin ever so lightly and lovingly and then sat on the floor near Myriam and Yosef. Myriam lay down in the straw and closed her eyes while Yosef spoke with Uriel.

"You were gone quite a while, Uriel. It must have been quite a distance to get your cloak. How did you manage in the dark?"

"Oh, at first there was enough light from the cave for me to see. But then when I got too far away, I could still see okay but I couldn't figure out how. Then I found a piece of straw from the cave stuck to my sleeve and I realized that somehow it must carry some of the cavelight. So, I was easily able to get back to where my sheep are and retrieve my aba for the baby. My brother was asleep, so I didn't wake him. I was nearly back here when I heard some men approaching on the road, so I hid amongst the rocks and bushes until they passed. It was there that I lost the piece of hay and its light. After that was when I hurt my arm and my knees and my toe until I got to where the cave-light was enough."

"You are quite a brave and industrious boy, Uriel. Your parents must be very proud of you. And you are able to figure things out on your own. That's very good. But you are wrong about the straw from the cave. It was not the straw that provided you with the light, it was you. When you touched my son, his light became part of you. It stayed with you all the while until you hid. When you hid his light—your light—from those men, you extinguished it. The light, once bestowed, is meant to be shared. When you keep it just for yourself it will go out. This child is a child of God, God's child. God's light dwells in him and now God's light dwells in you as well. You also are a child of God. He gave you all the light you need for your journey through life. Share the light, Uriel. Never let it go out.

"I know you'd like to stay but you need to return to your brother. You know that when he awakes, he will be very worried. You have fulfilled your mission for now, but there is much more for you to do in the future. Use your light well, Uriel. Use your light well."

Uriel bid Myriam and Yosef goodbye and stroked the baby's cheek one last time before he left. He easily navigated his way back, seeming to almost float over the rocky stretches.

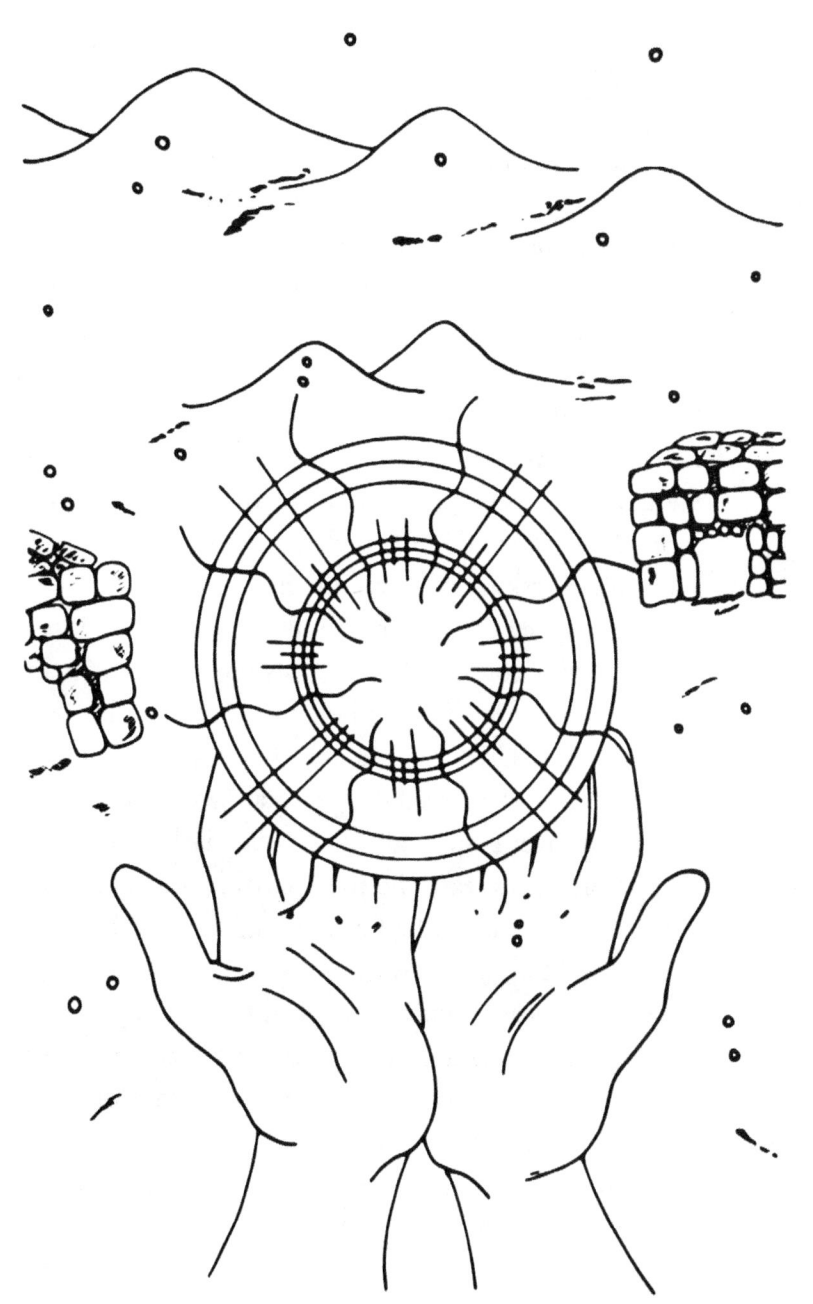

On the road, nearly to the cypress tree landmark, the quiet of the night was suddenly shattered by a loud noise, a cry, and an angry shout up ahead. Uriel's first instinct was to hide, but then he steeled himself and, with some trepidation, he forged onward. Shortly he came upon a man, moaning, sitting on a rock by the side of the road. The man's shattered lantern was there on the ground, blood was streaming down his face, and he seemed dazed. The man recoiled a bit when he saw Uriel and he let out a pitiful groan. It was obvious that the man had tripped, fallen, and struck his head on a rock. Uriel reassured him, washed the wound with water from his wineskin, and gave the man a drink. The cut was not that severe and after applying pressure on it for a while, Uriel got the bleeding to stop. Once the man regained his wits, he simply nodded thankfully and approvingly to Uriel but said not a word. Uriel gave him his wineskin and, assured that the man would be alright, bid the stranger good night. When he reached the trees and was about to leave the road, Uriel looked back and saw that the man now had just enough light of his own to shepherd him on his way.

As Uriel headed up to the pasture, he thought how he would be returning home without his aba, without his scrip, and without his wineskin, but with a lot more than what he left home with. He couldn't wait to reach his brother and tell him everything. But would Taoma believe him, or would he first need to go see for himself?

"I am the light of the world. Whoever follows me will not walk in darkness but will have the light of life."
—John 8:12

Acknowledgements

Who is to say where inspiration comes from? Certainly there is an entire lifetime of interactions with people who influence our lives and our thinking. The idea for this story rattled around in my head for several years before a word was typed into the computer. My parents were certainly a strong positive influence. I credit them with my faith. Certainly Yeshu was directing my fingers at the keyboard.

For this project, and all the diverse things that I do, whether writing, teaching Ukrainian Easter egg decorating, visiting some wonderful nonagenarians, doing a handyman project for someone, playing golf, participating in an investment club, or training for a marathon, I thank my wife for her constant support. It's so nice to have someone who will put up with my whims and allow me to be me.

The feedback on this story from my siblings was extremely helpful and enlightening. They not only identified numerous needed corrections to spelling and grammar, but pointed out inconsistencies, things they found confusing, and things they particularly liked. This was sometimes eye-opening to me as it demonstrated how different people can read the same thing but come away with opposite impressions. Regarding one particular scene I was praised by one person for the imagery while another basically commented that it did not make sense. I suppose sometimes in writing, or in any endeavor really, you just need to go with what feels right to you. But a special shout out to my brother; he put his critical literary eye to the story almost line by line and gave me a wealth of welcome feedback.

After committing to have this short story published I decided that, since it is religious in nature, I should have my pastor read it before proceeding too far. His feedback finalized my decision to publish it and I thank Rev. David C. Procaccini, Pastor of St. Francis de Sales, North Kingstown, Rhode Island for the beautiful foreword that he wrote.

For the illustrations I placed a request for an artist in my parish church bulletin and mentioned it at work. I thank those who sent me an example of their work. Just the fact that people were interested in participating in this endeavor warmed my heart. Having decided to include illustrations it dawned on me one day that I should really formalize the agreement between myself and the artist. My local library helped me find sample agreements, which I then used to create one that suited me. A dear friend was generous enough to put her legal eyes to it and offer suggestions.

I particularly want to thank Miranda Riccio who did the illustrations. There was something about her depiction of Uriel in the first illustration that spoke to me and ultimately led me to select her. Although we did not meet until after that, we worked extremely well together. I told her that I was inspired to write the words and I wanted the illustrations to reflect whatever inspiration came to her after reading the story; instead of being drawings dictated by me. Bravo Miranda!

And on the publishing side, Steve and Dawn at Stillwater River Publications were a pleasure to work with and made the entire process easy and enjoyable. Want to purchase this or any book? Support your local bookstore, like Stillwater Books.

About the Author

Tom is a retired engineer who has called Rhode Island home for the past 35 years. The son of a Byzantine Catholic father and a Roman Catholic mother, he has a foot in both rites. Tom has kept his Byzantine and eastern European heritage alive by carrying on traditions such as baking paska and kolach with recipes handed down through the generations. He has given a talk on the Byzantine rite to parishioners at his Roman Catholic parish, and holds classes on decorating Easter eggs in the Polish and Ukrainian styles. He is a weekly seasonal golfer, enjoys handyman work, has done some artwork in marquetry, and successfully completed the Tough Ruck marathon. Tom currently works part time for the Roman Catholic Diocese of Providence. This is Tom's first published work.

www.ingramcontent.com/pod-product-compliance
Lightning Source LLC
Chambersburg PA
CBHW070042070426
42449CB00012BA/3138